Bingo goes to school

Story by Annette Smith
Illustrations by Pat Reynolds

"Mom," said Sam.

"We are having a Pet Day
at school, on Saturday.
Can Bingo come to school?"

"Yes," said Mom.

"I will come and help you
look after him."

"Bingo," said Sam.

"You can come to school
with me on Saturday.
But you will have to be
a good dog."

Bingo jumped up at Sam.

"Sit, Bingo, sit," said Sam.
"Please be a good dog.
All the girls and boys
will be looking at you
on Pet Day."

"Walk with me, Bingo," said Sam.

"No, Bingo! No running!

Walk!

Mom! Look at Bingo!

He is not running.

He is walking with me."

On Pet Day,

Bingo went to school

with Sam and Mom.

They saw a little boy
with a black cat.

They saw two naughty dogs
running away.

Bingo looked at the cat.

"Woof!" said Bingo.

"Woof, woof, woof!"

"Stay here, Bingo," said Sam. **"Stay with me!"**

Bingo looked at the cat again, but he stayed with Sam.

"Bingo," said Sam.

"You are the best dog

at school, today."